❧ *This Book Belongs To* ❧

Name :

Phone :

Address :

Project Name :

Foreman :

Project No :

Date :

Day :

Visitors	Schedule

Problems	Safety Issues

Summary Of Work

Signature :

Employee	Trade	Hours	Overtime

Equipment On Site	No. Units

Materials Delivered	No. Units	Equipment Rented	Rate

Others

Notes :

Project Name :

Foreman :

Project No :

Date :

Day :

Visitors

Schedule

Problems

Safety Issues

Summary Of Work

Signature :

Employee	Trade	Hours	Overtime

Equipment On Site	No. Units

Materials Delivered	No. Units	Equipment Rented	Rate

Others

Notes :

Project Name : | Project No :
| Date :
Foreman : | Day :

Visitors

Schedule

Problems

Safety Issues

Summary Of Work

Signature :

Employee	Trade	Hours	Overtime

Equipment On Site	No. Units

Materials Delivered	No. Units	Equipment Rented	Rate

Others

Notes :

Project Name :

Foreman :

Project No :

Date :

Day :

Visitors

Schedule

Problems

Safety Issues

Summary Of Work

Signature :

Employee	Trade	Hours	Overtime

Equipment On Site	No. Units

Materials Delivered	No. Units	Equipment Rented	Rate

<table>
<tr><td align="center">Others</td></tr>
</table>

Notes :

Project Name :

Foreman :

Project No :

Date :

Day :

Visitors	Schedule

Problems	Safety Issues

Summary Of Work

Signature :

Employee	Trade	Hours	Overtime

Equipment On Site	No. Units

Materials Delivered	No. Units	Equipment Rented	Rate

Others

Notes :

Project Name :

Foreman :

| Project No : |
| Date : |
| Day : |

| Visitors | Schedule |

| Problems | Safety Issues |

Summary Of Work

Signature :

Employee	Trade	Hours	Overtime

Equipment On Site	No. Units

Materials Delivered	No. Units	Equipment Rented	Rate

Others

Notes :

Project Name :

Foreman :

Project No :

Date :

Day :

Visitors	Schedule

Problems	Safety Issues

Summary Of Work

Signature :

Employee	Trade	Hours	Overtime

Equipment On Site	No. Units

Materials Delivered	No. Units	Equipment Rented	Rate

Others

Notes :

Project Name : | Project No :
Date :
Foreman : | Day :

Visitors

Schedule

Problems

Safety Issues

Summary Of Work

Signature :

Employee	Trade	Hours	Overtime

Equipment On Site	No. Units

Materials Delivered	No. Units	Equipment Rented	Rate

Others

Notes :

Project Name :

Project No :

Date :

Foreman :

Day :

Visitors	Schedule

Problems	Safety Issues

Summary Of Work

Signature :

Employee	Trade	Hours	Overtime

Equipment On Site	No. Units

Materials Delivered	No. Units	Equipment Rented	Rate

Others

Notes :

Project Name :

Foreman :

Project No :

Date :

Day :

Visitors

Schedule

Problems

Safety Issues

Summary Of Work

Signature :

Employee	Trade	Hours	Overtime

Equipment On Site	No. Units

Materials Delivered	No. Units	Equipment Rented	Rate

Others

Notes :

Project Name :

Project No :

Date :

Foreman :

Day :

Visitors

Schedule

Problems

Safety Issues

Summary Of Work

Signature :

Employee	Trade	Hours	Overtime

Equipment On Site	No. Units

Materials Delivered	No. Units	Equipment Rented	Rate

Others

Notes :

Project Name :

Project No :

Date :

Foreman :

Day :

Visitors

Schedule

Problems

Safety Issues

Summary Of Work

Signature :

Employee	Trade	Hours	Overtime

Equipment On Site	No. Units

Materials Delivered	No. Units	Equipment Rented	Rate

Others

Notes :

Project Name :

Foreman :

Project No :

Date :

Day :

Visitors

Schedule

Problems

Safety Issues

Summary Of Work

Signature :

Employee	Trade	Hours	Overtime

Equipment On Site	No. Units

Materials Delivered	No. Units	Equipment Rented	Rate

Others

Notes :

Project Name :

Foreman :

Project No :

Date :

Day :

<table>
<tr><td>Visitors</td><td>Schedule</td></tr>
</table>

<table>
<tr><td>Problems</td><td>Safety Issues</td></tr>
</table>

Summary Of Work

Signature :

Employee	Trade	Hours	Overtime

Equipment On Site	No. Units

Materials Delivered	No. Units	Equipment Rented	Rate

Others

Notes :

Project Name :

Project No :

Date :

Foreman :

Day :

Visitors	Schedule

Problems	Safety Issues

Summary Of Work

Signature :

Employee	Trade	Hours	Overtime

Equipment On Site	No. Units

Materials Delivered	No. Units	Equipment Rented	Rate

Others

Notes :

Project Name :

Foreman :

Project No :

Date :

Day :

Visitors	**Schedule**

Problems	**Safety Issues**

Summary Of Work

Signature :

Employee	Trade	Hours	Overtime

Equipment On Site	No. Units

Materials Delivered	No. Units	Equipment Rented	Rate

<table>
<tr><td align="center">Others</td></tr>
</table>

Notes :

Project Name : _______________________________________

Foreman : _______________________________________

| Project No : |
| Date : |
| Day : |

Visitors

Schedule

Problems

Safety Issues

Summary Of Work

Signature : _______________________________

Employee	Trade	Hours	Overtime

Equipment On Site	No. Units

Materials Delivered	No. Units	Equipment Rented	Rate

Others

Notes :

Project Name :

Foreman :

Project No :

Date :

Day :

Visitors

Schedule

Problems

Safety Issues

Summary Of Work

Signature :

Employee	Trade	Hours	Overtime

Equipment On Site	No. Units

Materials Delivered	No. Units	Equipment Rented	Rate

Others

Notes :

Project Name :

Foreman :

Project No :

Date :

Day :

Visitors

Schedule

Problems

Safety Issues

Summary Of Work

Signature :

Employee	Trade	Hours	Overtime

Equipment On Site	No. Units

Materials Delivered	No. Units	Equipment Rented	Rate

<table><tr><td align="center">Others</td></tr></table>

Notes :

Project Name :

Project No :

Date :

Foreman :

Day :

Visitors

Schedule

Problems

Safety Issues

Summary Of Work

Signature :

Employee	Trade	Hours	Overtime

Equipment On Site	No. Units

Materials Delivered	No. Units	Equipment Rented	Rate

<table>
<tr><td>Others</td></tr>
</table>

Notes :

Project Name :

Foreman :

Project No :

Date :

Day :

Visitors	Schedule

Problems	Safety Issues

Summary Of Work

Signature :

Employee	Trade	Hours	Overtime

Equipment On Site	No. Units

Materials Delivered	No. Units	Equipment Rented	Rate

Others

Notes :

Project Name :

Foreman :

Project No :

Date :

Day :

<table>
<tr><td colspan="1">Visitors</td><td>Schedule</td></tr>
</table>

Visitors

Schedule

Problems

Safety Issues

Summary Of Work

Signature :

Employee	Trade	Hours	Overtime

Equipment On Site	No. Units

Materials Delivered	No. Units	Equipment Rented	Rate

Others

Notes :

Project Name : ______________________________________

Foreman : ______________________________________

Project No :

Date :

Day :

<table>
<tr><td>

Visitors

</td><td>

Schedule

</td></tr>
</table>

<table>
<tr><td>

Problems

</td><td>

Safety Issues

</td></tr>
</table>

Summary Of Work

Signature : ______________________________________

Employee	Trade	Hours	Overtime

Equipment On Site	No. Units

Materials Delivered	No. Units	Equipment Rented	Rate

<table><tr><td align="center">Others</td></tr></table>

Notes :

Project Name :

Project No :

Date :

Foreman :

Day :

Visitors

Schedule

Problems

Safety Issues

Summary Of Work

Signature :

Employee	Trade	Hours	Overtime

Equipment On Site	No. Units

Materials Delivered	No. Units	Equipment Rented	Rate

Others

Notes :

Project Name :

Foreman :

Project No :

Date :

Day :

Visitors

Schedule

Problems

Safety Issues

Summary Of Work

Signature :

Employee	Trade	Hours	Overtime

Equipment On Site	No. Units

Materials Delivered	No. Units	Equipment Rented	Rate

Others

Notes :

Project Name :

Foreman :

Project No :

Date :

Day :

Visitors

Schedule

Problems

Safety Issues

Summary Of Work

Signature :

Employee	Trade	Hours	Overtime

Equipment On Site	No. Units

Materials Delivered	No. Units	Equipment Rented	Rate

Others

Notes :

Project Name :

Foreman :

Project No :

Date :

Day :

Visitors

Schedule

Problems

Safety Issues

Summary Of Work

Signature :

Employee	Trade	Hours	Overtime

Equipment On Site	No. Units

Materials Delivered	No. Units	Equipment Rented	Rate

Others

Notes :

Project Name :

Foreman :

Project No :

Date :

Day :

Visitors

Schedule

Problems

Safety Issues

Summary Of Work

Signature :

Employee	Trade	Hours	Overtime

Equipment On Site	No. Units

Materials Delivered	No. Units	Equipment Rented	Rate

Others

Notes :

Project Name :

Foreman :

Project No :

Date :

Day :

Visitors

Schedule

Problems

Safety Issues

Summary Of Work

Signature :

Employee	Trade	Hours	Overtime

Equipment On Site	No. Units

Materials Delivered	No. Units	Equipment Rented	Rate

Others

Notes :

Project Name :

Foreman :

| Project No : |
| Date : |
| Day : |

Visitors

Schedule

Problems

Safety Issues

Summary Of Work

Signature :

Employee	Trade	Hours	Overtime

Equipment On Site	No. Units

Materials Delivered	No. Units	Equipment Rented	Rate